A Peaceable Classroom:
Activities to Calm and Free Student Energies

Merrill Harmin
and
Saville Sax

Winston Press

Winston Press, Inc.
430 Oak Grove
Minneapolis, MN 55403

Illustrated by Joe Loverti

Quotes on pages 11 and 123 used by permission of Argus Communications, copyright © 1974.

Quotes on pages 16 and 31 from the *Home Book of Quotations*, rev. ed. by Burton E. Stevenson, copyright © 1967 by Dodd, Mead & Company, Inc.

Quote on page 12 from the *Home Book of American Quotations*, selected and arranged by Bruce Bohle, copyright © 1967 by Dodd, Mead & Company, Inc.

A peaceable classroom, family, or work group flows harmoniously. Although disposed toward peace, a peaceable group is not always peaceful. Tension and conflict sometimes arise, as they inevitably do in nature. But in a peaceable classroom such anxious energies soon blend with a larger stream of accord, harmony, and support.

A peaceable classroom, like a forest, vibrates with aliveness and balance.

A group becomes more peaceable when its members learn how to free and calm their individual energies. In return, individual energies become more free and calm when persons live in a peaceable group.

Table of Contents

1. What this book is all about 1
    Our focus 2
    Who could use this book 4
    Usefulness in the classroom 5
    In brief 6

2. Activities for discharging tensions and freeing energies ... 9
    Activity 1: Deep breathing in preparation for work 13
    Activity 2: Complete breathing 14
    Activity 3: Stretching and shaking 17
    Activity 4: Scrunching the body to relax 19
    Activity 5: Tensing and relaxing muscles
                to relax the body 21
    Activity 6: Using the body sequence to relax the body... 23
    Activity 7: Learning to dissolve tension by giving in to it . 25

3. Activities for clearing the mind 29
    Activity 8: Mind-clearing 33
    Activity 9: A moment apart 35
    Activity 10: What's on your mind? 37
    Activity 11: The memory trip 38
    Activity 12: Clearing emotional energy 40

4. Activities for relaxing consciousness 45
    Activity 13: Seeing with new eyes 49
    Activity 14: Counting breaths 50
    Activity 15: Repeating a mantra to neutralize thoughts ... 52

5. Activities for centering the self 59
    Activity 16: Here and now wheel 63
    Activity 17: Enlarging awareness 65
    Activity 18: Breathing to regain the center of the self 67
    Activity 19: Rediscovering the whole self 69
    Activity 20: The listening activity 71
    Activity 21: The dream exchange 73

6. Activities for giving the self messages 77
    Activity 22: Sending general messages 80
    Activity 23: The fantasy story 83
    Activity 24: Side-stepping negative energy.............. 84
    Activity 25: Your own experimentation 87

7. Some questions we have heard
   and answers we have given............................. 93

8. An occasion to reassess one's teaching 109
    Learning support groups 110
    Group planning sessions 113
    Learning projects 115

9. Applications to counseling 119

10. About resources 125

Bibliography 126

A Personal Log 128

1

What this book is all about

For a long time now our eye has been on the world around us Our task has been to manage the environment, especially to extract from it plenty of food and shelter. And we have learned and taught our children much about that task: how plants grow, how machines work, what our history has been, and how to keep records of it all.

The management of *personal* problems has been much less of a concern to us. Yet we have learned and taught some things about that, such as how to resolve conflicts, what makes for effective organization, how to screen propaganda, and what games people are apt to play with each other.

We have attended least of all to those aspects of personal problems that are more internal than they are external, that deal more with inner processes than with outer relationships. Note how little we know about how to relax when we are upset, what to do when different parts of us want different things, how to stick to the decisions we make, how to develop and use our intuitions, and how to control our most ornery impulses. When it comes to such subjective realities, we have learned and taught our children relatively little. For which we pay a price.

Many of us could use help with what might be called inner management skills.

Consider, for example, a student who one morning thinks ahead to a test that looms large for him and whose insides quickly fill with fears. Not knowing what to do with those fears, he tries to put them aside. But the energy around the fears and the effort to hold them in place is distracting. So, he does particularly poorly in school that day; he is irritable with his friends at lunch; he picks on his sister in the evening; and he has strange, scary dreams that night. Yet the next day he awakens to find his test fears no easier to deal with. All that distress improved his situation not one bit.

Our student would have done better to handle his fears more directly and appropriately, but that would have required some skills that he probably has not yet learned.

1

Or consider this quote from a young woman, recently abandoned by her boyfriend:

I would make columns listing what I could do with my life. In each column I would list the pros and cons. It seemed like a good idea at the time and it eased my mind for a while, but in the long run it didn't help at all. I couldn't make decisions. Something was going on at a deeper level inside me and it had nothing to do with those lists. I couldn't do a thing.

Not having skills to deal with "deeper" processes, she was stuck. And she was convinced that she either had to remain stuck or turn to a psychiatrist for professional help. Her choices seem lamentably narrow.

The time has come to help people learn to do better with their internal processes. We believe that many persons are crying for such help. Increasingly, today's search is the search for inner peace.

Not that we believe we should discontinue work on problems outside the person. But we can work concurrently on better managing the world around us and the world within us. It may even be argued that we must do both. After all, we do not deal very creatively with our surroundings when our own insides twist and turn distractingly.

Our focus

Which brings us to this book. Our concern is with aspects of life that are essentially personal, subjective, and internal—particularly with the problems we all have with the flow of our thoughts and feelings.

Sometimes, of course, our thoughts and feelings flow comfortably and unselfconsciously and we live peaceful days. At other times, the flow is strained or stormy. Our insides clash or buzz nonproductively. We feel anxious, uncentered, blocked, unsure, ambivalent, or detached from parts of ourselves. In this state students cannot learn well, adults cannot teach well, and no one can relate with others very well.

2

Our concern is to reduce the frequency and duration of such states. Our question is: What can each of us do to calm those upsets we so commonly experience in life, and to free our energies for more productive and pleasurable pursuits? We might note here that we do not presume by this book to eliminate all the problems of the human predicament, nor to treat severe individual dysfunctions. We are not in the range of the physician treating serious illnesses. We are rather in the range of the educator instructing on habits of cleanliness, diet, and exercise necessary to maintain the flow of good health and to ease everyday maladies. We are looking for relatively simple skills we all can use to keep our inner lives flowing more easily, richly, and happily.

To be specific, this book includes five sets of activities you might want to try.

Discharging tensions and freeing energies

Modern life has a way of leaving a residue of noise inside us. A variety of tensions pile up and often we do not even know what they are. Sometimes we are not even aware that we feel an urge to settle our insides, or to calm that noise, or to vent whatever is rattling in our minds or muscles. When we have done something that releases the tensions, we remark how much better and more relaxed we feel. Chapter two presents activities for discharging the everyday tensions of life so that our energies may flow freely, smoothly, calmly, and fully.

Clearing the mind

Sometimes life is hectic or we live fast and become confused. Our minds get cluttered. Our priorities get lost. Our thinking gets sticky. Chapter three contains activities to help us clear our minds.

Relaxing consciousness

Our awareness sometimes gets blocked into a narrow channel.
We may lose touch with our imaginations, or our artistic senses,
or our wisest intuitions. We may be obsessed by the parts and
lose sight of the whole. In chapter four, we consider some
activities that can relax our minds and free awareness to flow
more comprehensively.

Centering the self

To be centered is to be whole, solid, strong. In a crazy-quilt
world, it is easy to become uncentered, fractured, insecure, out
of balance. Activities to help us regain our centers are presented
in chapter five.

Giving the self messages

Society is full of complicated, contradictory, and not always
kindly messages. Some of these we absorb uncritically. Then our
thinking becomes confused. We lose trust in ourselves, and
think thoughts that undermine us. But where and how do we
learn to sort out which of these messages to accept and which to
ignore? And where do we learn how to give ourselves the
messages we decide are best for us? Chapter six considers
activities for enabling us to give ourselves positive and helpful
messages.

Who could use this book

You could use this handbook of activities by yourself in trying to
develop internal management skills on your own. However,
most of us find it easier to work with others, either with a

partner or in a small, supportive group. In that way, we can help and encourage one another.

If you have a leader or instructor to guide you and support you—and sometimes to prod you—progress will probably be easiest of all. Recognizing that most persons will need such support, we have written the book from the perspective of a group leader. You will see that our activities are in the form of instructions such leaders might give group members.

And since we are especially interested in helping schools do more with the development of inner skills, we have phrased our instructions in such a way that teachers can use them in talking with students. If you are a leader of a different kind of group, simply rephrase those instructions to better suit your situation. And if you are using this book without a leader, please alter the language so that it speaks directly to you. Scan the book and you will see how to do this.

Usefulness in the classroom

We have been trying this book's activities in schools; and we are finding that teachers can readily use them in ordinary classrooms and that, when they do, the results are generally positive. Anxieties of students are reduced and student concentration is improved. Learning seems to increase. Our classroom exercises also tend to increase the comfort level of classroom climates and to make teaching itself a more pleasant occupation. Classrooms become more peaceable and productive. And no undesirable side effects are reported.

If these findings are substantiated and if these activities come to be used more widely, it may be a case of the right medicine at the right time. For we suspect that children, like adults, are increasingly absorbing the disquiet of our times and that, again like adults, children increasingly need something to help them transpose that disquiet into a more productive and creative energy. If you are a teacher, this book should help you test the possibility that you can meet that need in your classroom.

In brief

The activities in this book are based on the assumption that we can make decisions to influence the tones and colors of our feelings and the flow and depth of our intelligence. We can learn to influence our inner processes much like we learn to influence the processes of things around us. We can therefore learn how to be ourselves and use ourselves in this world more fully, more effectively, and more joyfully.

Approach this book experimentally. Look it over. Pick one of the activities that appeals to you and with which you feel at least a little comfortable. Try the activity on yourself to get the feel of it. Then try it on your group, adjusting the language and the tempo to make it fit your situation.

Like anything new, the first few times you try an activity you may feel awkward. But you will get the hang of it. And by trying you will see what, if anything, an activity does for your group.

If you are like most teachers, you won't want to use all the book's activities. But, by experimenting a bit, you should find at least some that you won't want to live without and that help you do your job with more peace of mind, more flexibility, and more delight.

Man cannot discover
new oceans
unless he has courage
to lose sight
of the shore.

Andre Gide

2
Activities for discharging tensions and freeing energies

Sometimes we have a bad day or a hectic day and we get stuck in our tensions. The tensions somehow do not leave us. Our insides get clogged and we can't easily relax, use our intelligence, or interact calmly and productively. Or sometimes nothing special happens but, usually unknowingly, we have accumulated so much tension from life that our energies become clogged and sluggish. Our tightness blocks our powers. When that happens, we need to call on activities that free us from those tensions, that help the tensions get out of us, that allow our fullest and most healthy energies to flow again.
For teachers, it is a problem to have on hand activities that free students from special tensions or anxieties or that simply allow them to escape the normal pressures accumulated from society and to move into a space that is more open and nourishing, more peaceful and productive, so that students can learn more easily and interact more calmly.

   The seven activities in this chapter serve such purposes. Try some of those with which you feel most comfortable.

Activities for discharging tensions might be useful—

—whenever a group first meets;
—when a group becomes hyperactive;
—when controversy has raised the group's emotional
   temperature too high;
—when a student is upset and wants to regain control.

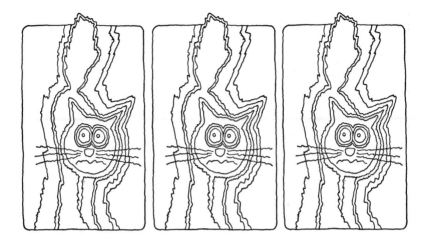

When I hide my emotions,
my stomach keeps score.

Self-trust is the first
secret of success.

Ralph Waldo Emerson

Activity 1
Deep breathing in preparation for work

1. Let's try a settling-in exercise before we begin our work. This exercise might help some of us to relax. Sit comfortably. Then close your eyes. Notice your breathing. *(Pause)* Notice how your breath is coming in and going out. *(Pause)*

2. Now breathe deeply and slowly. Sit straight. Let your breath be deep and natural. *(Pause a little longer.)* Breathe deeply and smoothly. *(Pause)*

3. Now become aware of your body and let it relax. Let your whole body become easy. *(Pause)*

4. Continue until you are easy and relaxed; then, when you are ready, open your eyes slowly and we'll begin our work. *(Pause until most eyes are open and proceed with the group's work.)*

Note: In place of step four, you might occasionally try the following ending:

Think how you want to be when you open your eyes. Do you want to be alert and ready to work? Do you want to be able to remember what you will read? Imagine yourself being just the way you want yourself to be. When you get your image clear and strong, open your eyes.

Activity 2
Complete breathing

1. Let's try some complete breathing today to help us get settled and energized.
    Sit comfortably. Sit up straight. Sit solidly in your chair, feet flat on the floor. Close your eyes or keep them open, whichever you prefer.

2. With one hand on your abdomen below your waistline and the other hand on your chest, breathe in and pull some air into your abdomen.
    Now gradually pull air into your chest to fully inflate your lungs.

3. Hold this position for a short while. Then gradually, smoothly, let the air out and relax.

4. Try steps 2 and 3 again. We're trying for what we call a complete breath. Breathe air into your abdomen; then gradually pull air into your chest. Hold this position. Gradually let the air out. *(Repeat and re-explain as necessary.)*

5. Now do this exercise on your own with smooth rhythm. Count to yourself: air in— 1,2,3,4; hold it— 1,2,3,4; air out— 1,2,3,4. Try to do all the steps smoothly. Remember that the "air-in" step starts with air deep in the abdomen; by the count of 4 the air should fill all your lungs. *(If necessary, demonstrate the counting in front of the class.)*

6. After three or four of these complete breaths, you should be feeling stronger and calmer. Try this type of complete breathing and then we'll begin our work.

Note: Some students will be able to extend the second two stages beyond four counts. This is good. A rhythm of 4-6-6 is usually more energizing and relaxing than a rhythm of 4-4-4. After students have had some experience with complete breathing, encourage those who can do so to extend the "hold-it" and "air-out" steps to a count of 6, or even to 8, if they can do so comfortably.

A word about breathing—

Many students do not know how to breathe deeply. As a consequence, they often lose access to their deepest energies. So we sometimes play a little demonstration game with students:

"Watch me breathe in a quick, shallow fashion. See my chest go in and out fast and my shoulders go up and down. Now try it yourself. Put your hand on your chest and breathe quickly and shallowly.

"Put your other hand on your abdomen below your waistline. Now try to breathe by keeping your chest quiet and pulling the air in from your abdomen. Try to balloon out your abdomen. That's the way singers and athletes have to breathe to do a good job. Practice until you can breathe that way—deeply, smoothly, and fully."

We sometimes ask students to keep one hand on their chests and the other hand on their abdomens ("stomachs") whenever they do Activity 1, to help them identify deep breathing. It's also a useful posture for learning Activity 2.

As long as you live,
keep learning
how to live.

Lucius Anneus Seneca

Activity 3
Stretching and shaking

1. Stand up and take a breath or two.

2. Shake your shoulders. Shake off your cares and woes. Loosen up your neck area.

3. Reach for the ceiling. Reach as high as you can. Stretch your body tall. Hold this position.

4. Bring your arms down and relax. Do a bit more shaking. Try shaking the center of your body.

5. Reach for the ceiling again. Stretch yourself up there. Relax.

6. Bend and reach for the floor. Don't strain; go as far as you can easily. Bounce around a little.

7. By yourself now, without bothering those around you, do more shaking and stretching and bending until you feel loose and easy. Then sit and we'll get ready for our work.

If you cannot
find it in yourself,
where will you go for it?

an ancient Chinese proverb

Activity 4
Scrunching the body to relax

1. Close your eyes. Then scrunch up your whole body—holding all your muscles as tightly as you can—your neck, face, legs, arms, stomach. Pull your whole body in and make it tight around you. Hold this position briefly.

2. Then let it all go, relax, open up your body, and take a few slow deep breaths.

3. Again, tighten up all your body—all the muscles in your body. Bend over and pull up your legs and tighten up your fists. Hold this position.

4. Now let go. Release it all. Relax. Breathe slowly.

5. Again, tighten your whole body. Hold your body tight. Hold it. Now let go. Let all your tensions go.

6. Release and relax. Feel all your energy flowing comfortably. Breathe easily. Get yourself settled and ready for work.

One teacher says—

"I find that students get all tight and nervous when they take a test, even when the test is just a learning exercise. Many get tight heads, cramped hands. Some get headaches. So, after I give a test, I have the students relax any muscles that they find are tight. That makes them much more relaxed when it's time to correct their work and more ready to learn something."

Activity 5
Tensing and relaxing muscles
to relax the body

1. Close your eyes. Let your attention flow into your body.

2. When you feel tension in a certain area, direct energies to that area. Tighten up the muscles in that area; gradually increase the energy until you are holding the muscles as tightly as you can. Hold this position briefly. Then release. Let the muscles relax and stretch.

3. Repeat this tense-relax process, in the same area of your body or another, until you feel relaxed all over. *(Pause until most seem to stop tensing and relaxing.)*

4. When you are relaxed, open your eyes and we'll begin work.

Note: You may want to suggest to the students that they use this activity whenever they want to relax their bodies.

A further thought—

Choosing to flow with, not against, life's forces is usually the wisest course. Consider the force of anger. When we deny that force within us, it remains to contaminate our beings for long periods of time. When we let the anger flow, when we open ourselves to the energy of the anger and feel it and express it, its force dissipates naturally and readily, and we become free of it.

So also with tensions. Tensions have a force to them and we pay a price if we do not flow with that force. Choose to attend to your tensions, not to ignore them. Direct energies to them, not elsewhere. Do not attempt to override your tensions or distract yourself from them. Let your energies flow with your tensions without thinking or judging. Just be aware of the tensions and let them flow. You will be more quickly released from their force and become easy with yourself.

Activity 6
Using the body sequence to relax the body

1. Look around to see that all is well around you. Then close your eyes. Sit up straight, feet on the floor. Sit firm in your chair, hands comfortably in your lap.

2. Tense the muscles in your feet and legs as tightly as you can. Hold this position. Then release and stretch those muscles. *(Pause as necessary.)*

3. Now go to the center of your body, around your stomach. Tighten up some muscles there. Hold these muscles tight. Release and relax these muscles.

4. Now go to your shoulders and neck. Tighten up muscles in that area. Hold this position. Release and relax those muscles.

5. Now tighten the muscles of your hands and arms. Hold them tight. Release and relax those muscles.

6. Now tighten your face muscles. If you like, make a real face. Hold your face muscles tight. Release.

7. When you are easy, refreshed, and ready for work, open your eyes and we'll begin our class.

Note: Watch the group to get the rhythm of this activity. You will see when most students have relaxed and are ready for the next step.

You can make the activity richer by making the body trip longer and more detailed. A very detailed trip would have the tense-release sequence applied separately to toes, whole foot, ankles, calves, thighs, hips, stomach, chest, shoulders, neck, upper arms, hands, fingers, eyes, forehead area, back of head, jaws, lips.

A further thought—

You can't appreciate good food just by looking at it; nor can you truly assess the impact of the activities in this book by merely reading them. We encourage you to try them on yourself before deciding if they will be valuable in your classroom. Or, have someone read the directions for a specific activity to you while you act the part of a student doing the activity. This will help you get the feel of the activity and prepare you to find comfortable language for yourself and your group. It will also help you to use these activities more artistically than mechanically.

We would not recommend that you assess the activities after just one trial with a group. We often require time before we become accustomed to new things. If an activity seems to have some promise of serving your purposes, try it three times, with as much confidence as you can bring to it, before deciding whether or not it is helpful.

Incidentally, we like to get data from students to help us decide if we should keep an activity in our repertoire. Often we end a new activity with a question such as "Did anyone get anything good from that activity?"

Activity 7
Learning to dissolve tension by giving in to it

Note: Because this activity often makes a person aware of some distress or tension, use it only in climates that are trusting and supportive.

1. Close your eyes. Take a few deep breaths. Think of something that is bothering you. Anything bothering you is okay to think of. Give a name to that bothersome thing and say its name in your head.

2. As you repeat this name, tension will probably show up in some areas of your body. Focus your attention on a tense area while continuing to repeat the name of the bothersome thing in your head. Now tighten the muscles in that tense area. Hold the muscles tight. Relax.

3. Continue tightening and relaxing in that tense area, or in any other part of your body, at your own rhythm.

4. Continue until saying the name of your bothersome thing produces no more tension inside you and you feel free and relaxed.

Also use the following activities to help discharge tensions—

—Encourage your students to write or talk about the bothersome issues inside them. Perhaps use a suggestion box for this.

—Model or role play someone who blows off steam without creating tension in someone else. Express your own distresses nondestructively. Talk about the feelings within you rather than about the causes of those feelings.

—Permit students to complain, to cry, to smash one hand into the other, to giggle, or to shiver if that will help them discharge their tensions. Sometimes let them vent their negative feelings in small groups.

—Let students walk about or talk if that will help release tensions.

—Help students obtain sufficient exercise and play.

—When tensions are mounting, use and encourage the use of humor, even silliness.

—Reduce tensions by reducing the factors that energize them: fears of failure, trying to live up to others' expectations, intense competition, and so on.

**Use the following questions to evaluate the success
of the tension-discharging activities—**

—Do the suggested exercises enable you to help your students
more quickly dissolve tensions that they bring in from
elsewhere?

—Do the tension-discharging activities help you more quickly
dissolve tensions that arise during the class?

—Do students appear generally more relaxed and ready for
learning after you have used the suggested exercises?

—Are frowns less often in evidence and smiles more frequent
following these activities?

—Do students say that they enjoy the activities?

—Do students report that they have used these exercises out of
class or taught them to others?

—After the students have used these exercises for a while, are
there fewer instances when an irritable student disturbs the
class?

—Is there a more friendly atmosphere?

28

3
Activities for clearing the mind

We sometimes get stuck in inaction or confusion because of too-muchness or too-fastness—too many distractions, too many thoughts, too many worries, too many curiosities. The overload constricts us. Our minds have no space in which to move.

This chapter contains activities that assist us in uncluttering our minds, in regaining our perspectives, and in clarifying our priorities. The activities allow our intellectual energies to flow more richly. They are especially useful before important thinking, for they clear out space in which new thoughts can flow.

You may not wish to try all of the activities in this chapter, but see if you can get some to work for you.

Activities for clearing the mind might be useful—

—for three or four minutes at the beginning of each session;
—between activities;
—around holidays and special occasions;
—when students feel confused or in conflict;
—when students have lost perspective on an issue.

Why seek you for your felicity abroad, which is placed within yourself?

Boethius

Quiet minds cannot be perplexed
or frightened,
but go on in fortune or misfortune
at their own private pace,
like a clock in a thunderstorm.

Robert Louis Stevenson

Activity 8
Mind-clearing

1. Sit relaxed, comfortably, with eyes open or closed, as you prefer. Take a few deep breaths.

2. Allow thoughts to come and go. Do not pay close attention to the thoughts that come. Do not study them. Do not work at them. But, also, do not ignore them. Just be aware of the thoughts that come to you.

3. Continue until the thoughts stop coming and your mind is more clear. *(Two to four minutes is usually enough.)* At this time your breathing should be more relaxed. You should also have a pleasant sense of well-being.

Note: Suggest to the students that they use this mind-clearing exercise whenever they wish to get ready for something new. Tell them to let their thoughts flow naturally until their minds are clear.

A further thought—

Repressed thoughts tie us up in much the same way that repressed feelings do. When we want to clear our minds and release our energies, we do well first to let our thoughts settle themselves. If we let these thoughts exist and move about at random without being judged as good or bad, positive or negative, worthy or unworthy, they will soon be ready to pass or settle and leave us more free.

Activity 9
A moment apart

1. Take a few moments to close your eyes and relax. Perhaps put your head on your arms. Let your mind clear itself. (*Gentle music from a record player or tape recorder is often helpful at this point.*)

2. (*After a suitable interlude, lower the music and speak softly.*) Bring yourself back to us now, slowly and easily. If you like, stretch the skin on your face by opening your eyes and mouth widely a few times.

3. Now let's begin our work.

From the moment of birth
we are immersed in action,
and can only fitfully guide it
by taking thought.

Alfred North Whitehead

Activity 10
What's on your mind?

1. What's on your mind? Take a piece of paper and make some notes, or draw some doodles, or write some words. Let your crayons or pencil say what's on your mind or inside your feelings. You won't have to share your work with others. Take just a moment to inventory what's inside of you. If you have nothing on your mind just now, draw aimlessly.

2. *(Follow up step 1 with one of the following options:)*
    —Well, it's good to clear our minds that way once in a while. You may want to go back and think more about what you noticed was inside you. Use your papers to remind you of what that was. But now let's get on with our work. *(Do not discuss what was on the students' minds.)*
    —Anyone want to share something that was on his or her mind? *(Encourage comments on the activity, and accept with thanks any comment made without feeling any need to elaborate or discuss it further. If time is limited, sample only a few students.)*
    —I'd be happy to hear later on from any of you about what was on your mind. Leave a note on my desk, or speak to me later if you like. But now let's take a few deep or complete breaths, relax, and get on with our work. *(Accept private communications on the activity.)*

Activity 11
The memory trip*

Note: The idea of this activity is to assist a person to relive in a leisurely manner an experience that was hectic or pressured, enabling the person to settle any loose ends in awareness and clear his or her mind. The memory trip is especially useful after emotionally-rich experiences. These directions, however, were written for use in the middle of an ordinarily busy day. We assume, of course, that you will change the wording to suit different circumstances.

1. Sit comfortably and look around a bit, if you like, to see that the space around you is secure. Relax, take a few deep breaths, and close your eyes.

2. Now imagine yourself the way you were when you woke up this morning. See yourself getting up and getting dressed. (*Pause*) Try to see some of the colors in your morning scene. (*Pause*)

3. Now try to relive your breakfast time. Can you see the scene? (*Pause*) Can you recapture any smells? Any sounds? (*Pause*)

4. Imagine now your trip to school. Experience yourself coming to school this morning. Try to capture the feelings you had. (*Pause*)

5. Now imagine the beginning of school. Review what happened and how you felt. Play out a little movie in your head. (*Pause*)

6. Continue to relive your day. Stop along the highlights of your day until this moment. Just let the images come and go until you have brought yourself up to date. (*Pause a little longer.*)

7. When you are ready, slowly, gently, at your own speed, open your eyes. Be here now with us. How many feel they settled some loose ends in their minds and are now more ready for work? Well, let's get to it.

*Special thanks to Tamaji Harmin for this activity.

Activity 12
Clearing emotional energy

1. Relax and place the tip of your index finger, the finger next to your thumb, on the desk. I'm going to call out a feeling and your job is first to feel that feeling and then to express the feeling with the tip of your finger in any way you wish. There is no right-wrong to this. In this activity you simply touch your desk with the tip of your finger to express a feeling. And we are not going to express our feelings in a big way. Keep the tip of your finger in a small space on your desk and express the feeling with your finger in any way that feels right to you.

2. Here's the first feeling—"anger." Try to feel anger. When you feel anger, let the tip of your finger express it in a small space on your desk top. Express the anger, then pause, then again express the anger with your finger, pause, and continue like that until I call out a new emotion. *(Pause)*

3. Thank you. Now try this feeling—"hate." Try to feel hate. When you can feel some hate, express that feeling with the tip of your finger in any way you wish.

4. Fine. Now try to feel "sadness." Express sadness with the tip of your finger in any way you want. *(If necessary, advise against any loud or large movements that distract others.)*

5. Now try "love." Express that with your finger tip.

6. Try "joy." Express joy with your finger tip. *(For each feeling, pause long enough for students to tune into the feeling and to express it at least five or ten times. You could tap your desk every five seconds or so and instruct students to give a new finger expression after each tap. You may consider adding, especially for older students: "sexuality," "reverence," and "no emotion.")*

40

7. We sometimes have emotions inside us that do not get
    fully expressed. This little activity helps us to tune into
    emotions and to clear ourselves of some of them, so
    we carry fewer loose ends around inside us. Anyone
    feel lighter after doing this activity?

Note: More than some other activities, this one requires
repetition before its benefits are fully obtained. Generally,
students get more from it after they have experienced it several
times. Note that the way the finger moves is unimportant; the
finger tip merely serves as a neutral focus for the expression of
emotional energy.

A comment on Activity 12—

Activity 12 is adapted from the work of Manfred Clynes. (For
research showing the benefits of regular use of the activity, see
his book *Sentics: The Touch of Emotions,* Doubleday, 1977.)
    It can be a strong activity. From time to time some students
will weep when the feeling of sadness or grief is experienced. At
other times, students will giggle from nervousness. We find it
important to protect such students and if such expressions occur
we announce that they are perfectly all right.
    We also find it useful to explain to students how our
emotions, when they are not expressed, can tie us up. Students
can usually appreciate how one can feel better after kicking a
can or otherwise expressing pent-up anger. Students who are
fully able to get into this activity often find a similar release. At
least, many say that they feel more light, free, and open.

Also use the following activities to help clear the mind—

—Give your students time to sit quietly and daydream, doodle, or draw aimlessly.
—Insert space between and around activities to provide moments of quiet and calm.
—Play music on a record player as students are gathering for class or before they leave.
—Have students look closely or aimlessly at nature, animals, art, and the outdoors to soothe and bring perspective to awareness.
—Welcome times when horseplay or casual conversations spring up.
—Provide for play with water, colors, shapes, or other sensuous materials.

Use the following questions to evaluate the success of the mind-clearing activities—

—Do mind-clearing procedures provide you with methods of calming students' minds so that the students are less often distracted and more fully attentive to learning?

—Do students say that mind-clearing procedures are useful to them?

—Do students report using mind-clearing activities outside of class or teaching them to others?

—Does mind-clearing give you a method for more quickly and easily settling a class after confusion or a loss of perspective has developed?

—Do you enjoy teaching more after using these procedures?

—After using these activities for a period of time, do students more frequently say positive things about your class?

—Have you observed an increase in creativity and spontaneity?

4
Activities for relaxing consciousness

Relaxing consciousness is the freeing of awareness so that our deepest senses and broadest insights are embraced.

Our awareness sometimes gets locked into a narrow channel. We become so busy accomplishing goals and avoiding problems that we lose touch with our imaginations, our artistic senses, our wisest intuitions, or our awareness of the wholeness of life. We may be obsessed by the parts and lose sight of the whole.

In this chapter we offer three activities that can relax our minds and free awareness to flow more comprehensively, more deeply, and more fully.

Activities for relaxing consciousness might be useful—

—once or twice each school day, preferably during late morning and midafternoon;

—once or twice on non-school days, preferably before mealtimes;

—when students are preparing themselves for a special challenge;

—whenever diffuse, unexplainable anxiety arises within a person.

The more faithfully
you listen
to the voice within you,
the better you will hear
what is sounding outside.

**One teacher, Valerie Meyer,
to whom we owe a special note of thanks
for the idea behind Activity 13, writes—**

"Newness becomes a great freeing up experience for me.
If 9 A.M. no longer exists, what do I have at 10:25? I have
only 10:25. When I could internalize this, I began to feel that all
experiences, situations, feelings, and learning have a true sense
of newness/nowness, a tremendous quality of freshness.
Obviously, everything happens only once in a never before or
again way. Realizing this makes almost everything fun and very
exciting.

"Some of the moments of joy I've experienced in the past
few days include—smelling bath soap, telling Sheri I'm glad
she's in my class (hearing she's glad, too), hugging, laughing,
making soup, being glad I'm here, making this year's Christmas
cards.

"Joy came to me when I saw, or felt, or heard—warm towels,
powder, the stillness of the morning, the lines of bare tree
branches against the sky, a sleeping cat on a most colorful
blanket, cloud and sky colors seen out of the kitchen window,
music, Ruth's childlike Christmas decorations, sounds of wind,
the air's clearness and crispness."

Activity 13
Seeing with new eyes

1. First stand up and stretch and shake your stiffness away. *(See Activity 3.)*

2. Now sit and look around you with new eyes as if you are seeing things for the very first time. Try to see things as if you have never seen them before. *(Pause)*

3. Who saw something with new eyes? *(Call on a few students to give examples of what they saw.)*

4. Try again to see with new eyes. Perhaps look at your hands, or your clothing, or things around the room. Try to see things as if you were seeing them for the very first time. *(Pause a little longer.)*

5. It's often a good idea to try to see with new eyes once each day—coming to school, in school, going home, anytime. See if that doesn't add new satisfaction to your days.

Activity 14
Counting your breaths

Note: Many people find breath counting makes them more peaceful and more energetic. They require less sleep and experience more satisfaction.

1. Sit securely with your back straight, feet flat on the floor. Close your eyes. Breathe in any way that is comfortable to you. (*Pause*) Become aware of your breath flowing in and flowing out of your nose.

2. In a moment I will ask you to count each breath—one as you take it in. Then exhale. Two as you breathe in again, and so on, up to ten. Then you will begin again, from one to ten and back to one again. Each time you feel your breath coming in count one.

3. When you notice that your mind has wandered and that you have forgotten to count, just begin again at one. Start counting whenever you have been distracted or your mind has wandered. Keep counting from one to ten and starting again at one.

4. Sometimes you will find that you have counted past ten and are up to fifteen or sixteen. That's okay. Just start back at one again whenever you notice you've gotten off the track.

5. Let's try it now for three minutes. Be aware of your breaths and start counting now, from one to ten. Count one as you breathe in, two as you breathe in again, and so on.

6. (*Pause for a minute or so.*) Be aware of your breathing. Focus on the air coming in and going out.

7. (*Pause another minute or so.*) Stay aware of your breathing.

8. The three minutes are now over; so slowly, at your own speed, open your eyes and come back to us. (*Pause until most are ready.*) Did this breath counting activity do anything good for anyone today?

9. Do this activity whenever you want to calm your thoughts and free your awareness. Counting your breaths twice a day, for ten or twenty minutes each session, will help keep your awareness moving comfortably and comprehensively within you. You will probably have to practice this many times before it becomes easy for you. This activity is like any sport or skill—it takes practice to be able to do it nicely. So stick with it.

Note: You might try breath counting for five minutes the second time you use this activity and, if the students stay with it, ten minutes the third time, and then turn it over to students to use on their own.

One teacher says—

"I tried breath counting with my biology classes yesterday. Today they wanted to start class again that way. They loved it!"

Activity 15
Repeating a mantra to neutralize thoughts

Note: This is a variant of Activity 14 and serves very similar purposes. After your group has experienced breath counting, you might introduce this as an alternative and suggest that some may wish to try it to see if it works better for them than breath counting. Usually we give all the directions more or less as they are outlined below, and then let students do the activity on their own. Some students may want to take notes and try the activity at home; others may wish to sit alone and do it during a quiet time in class.

1. Sit securely. Close your eyes. Repeat to yourself a word or phrase that sounds pleasant to your being. Consider one of the following mantras: water, om, clouds, one, sunshine.

2. Keep repeating your mantra in a way that is comfortable for you. Your silent sound may naturally repeat itself in synchronization with your breathing or your heartbeat. But it may also come irregularly and correspond to a rhythm that only you can imagine.

3. From time to time, your mind will wander. When this happens, simply begin again to repeat your word or phrase to yourself.

4. Continue repeating your mantra for five to twenty minutes or until your consciousness feels easy, free, content.

A further thought—

Intuitions, like emotions and thoughts, have their own forces. The forces of intuitions are for most of us quite faint, although they are sometimes strong enough to break into awareness. Even the busiest persons sometimes report inexplicable messages, often of dangers, rising as if from their instincts.

We suspect that intuitions, like emotions and thoughts, are best left to flow and to discharge their energies. And we suspect that the repeating of a mantra serves us nicely because the sound of that mantra dissipates our thought processes and thus provides more room for our intuitive processes to flow. The intuitive forces are thereby allowed to come alive and, after expressing themselves, to leave us free of their energies and more relaxed and open to life.

Perhaps repeating a mantra during the day works like dreaming at night to relieve us of certain real but unrecognized pressures.

One teacher says—

"I teach six and seven year olds. I gave them the word *owl* and told them to say that word to themselves while they played quietly or walked around. I said that *owl* was their word of wisdom and if they said it easily to themselves every once in a while it would make them wise. They liked the idea and many of them do it every day. Sometimes I remind them, but I don't insist that all do it and I never check up on it. I notice some students who seem to brighten after saying that word of wisdom to themselves. Some others seem to calm down better."

They are free
who do not fear
to go to the ends
of their thoughts.

Also use the following activities to help relax consciousness—

—Have your students close their eyes and listen to peaceful music.
—Ask students to identify with nature—for example, to feel like a tree, to be like the winds, to be a rock or a ray of light.
—Ask students to walk in an open area, such as a park or woods, and to daydream as they go.
—Ask students to relax and, for three or more minutes, to observe others who are working, walking, eating, or studying.
—Show abstract paintings or designs, perhaps as slides, and ask students to reflect on them silently.

**Use the following questions to evaluate the success
of the relaxing consciousness activities—**

—Do students who count breaths or repeat mantras report that
they are generally more relaxed and feel better?

—Do the students practicing the consciousness-relaxing
activities report that they need less sleep or are more
energetic?

—Is there evidence that students using these activities are more
healthy and less often sick or in need of medicine?

—After using these activities for a time, do students report that
they learn more easily and remember longer?

—Following the use of the consciousness-relaxing activities, do
students give evidence of being more cooperative, more
friendly?

—Are students who use these relaxing activities able to
concentrate for longer periods of time?

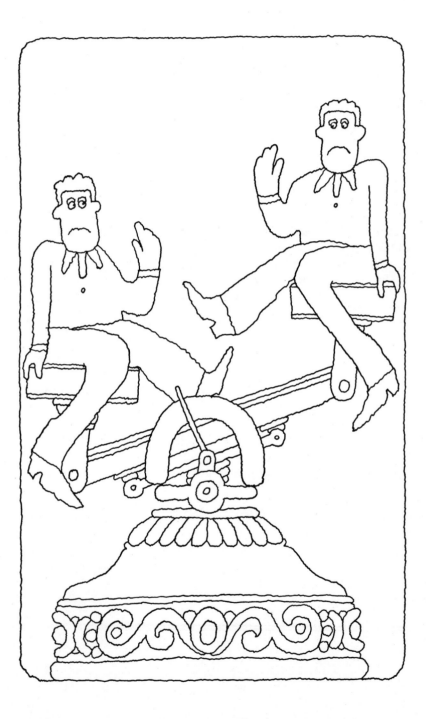

5
Activities for centering the self

Centering is the returning of awareness from distractions to the whole of oneself or to what is important to oneself.

To be centered is to be whole, solid, strong. In a crazy-quilt world, it is easy to become uncentered, fractured, insecure, out of balance.

Chapter 5 provides three activities to help us regain our centers.

Activities for centering the self might be useful—

—before an anxious event, as before report cards are
  distributed;
—whenever a group gathers, especially if the members live in
  distressing environments;
—when a person has lost balance or a sense of what is
  important;
—after a particularly hectic or stressful school experience.

I have no doubt whatever that most people live, whether physically, intellectually or morally, in a very restricted circle of their potential being. They make use of a very small portion of their possible consciousness, and of their soul's resources in general, much like a man who, out of his whole bodily organism, should get into a habit of using and moving only his little finger....

William James

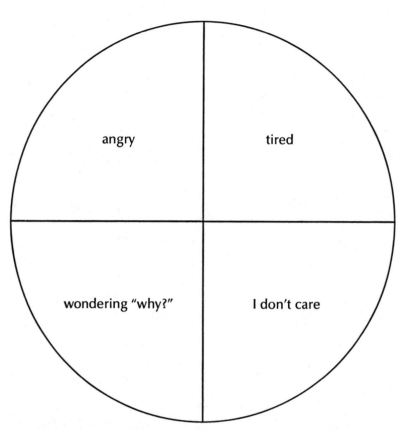

angry	tired
wondering "why?"	I don't care

I think this discussion is doing *no* good! All we are doing is hurting people. Including me.

_____

_____

_____

_____

_____

_____

_____

Activity 16
The here and now wheel

1. Take out a piece of paper and draw a circle large enough to write some words inside. (*Draw one yourself on the chalkboard.*)

2. Now divide the circle into four sections and, in each section, write or draw something that indicates a thought or feeling inside you right now. (*You might do this on the chalkboard too.*)

3. Now please take *one* of these items, any one, and expand on it. Perhaps you will want to write a sentence or two about it. (*You may also demonstrate this.*)

4. Would anyone be willing to share with all of us something you wrote? (*You might sample two or three students.*)

5. Perhaps we are now in touch with more of our whole selves. We might have better balance. Let's continue our work and see if this helps us in any way. (*Or, you might at this point ask students to form groups of two or three and to share parts of their wheels with each other. This would assist students in understanding what was going on inside others.*)

Note: This activity is especially useful when a discussion gets too heated or whenever students have lost touch with their whole selves.

People are disturbed not by things,
but by the views which they take of them.

Epictetus

Activity 17
Enlarging awareness

Note: This activity is useful when students get over-excited, argumentative, anxious, very bored, depressed, or saddened.

1. Let's stop a moment and get in touch with our full selves. Please close your eyes. Sit comfortably. Take a few deep breaths. Allow whatever comes to you to come. Be aware of what comes to you right now. (*Pause for several moments.*)

2. What sensations are you aware of right now? (*Pause*) Sounds? (*Pause*) Heat or cold? (*Pause*) The chair and the earth holding up your body? (*Pause for several moments.*)

3. What thoughts or feelings come to your awareness? Let them come and let them go. Experience the flow of your awareness as fully as you can. (*Pause*)

4. What else comes to your awareness? Take a few deep breaths again and let your insides settle in any way they want to. (*Pause*)

5. You should now be more centered. More of your whole self should be flowing comfortably. You can probably think better. When you are ready, slowly open your eyes and come back to our group.

6. All of us lose touch with our full selves from time to time. When that happens, take a moment to relax and open your awareness this way. A procedure such as we just used will help you do that. It will put you in contact with all the wisdom inside you.

A further thought—

Being uncentered is being detached from parts of ourselves. Parts of us are not active in the processes of the moment. Thus, our thinking, feeling, or perceiving is incomplete or distorted. Having turned off parts of ourselves, we feel uncentered or unbalanced and often vulnerable to danger.

This state is usually accompanied by noticeable changes in the breathing processes. We struggle to think of a word and we catch our breath. We become fearful and our breathing becomes shallow and quick. Breathing thus reflects our state of being. Constrained breathing is associated with constrained being. Full, relaxed breathing is associated with full, relaxed being.

When we want to escape a constrained state—generally, the physical sensation is one of being tight—we can start by breathing more slowly and deeply. Somehow that signals our life processes to flow more fully and richly. We can thus turn ourselves toward a more fully functioning state whenever we choose to do so.

Once you have experienced centering, you can become somewhat recentered simply by recalling imaginatively the experience of regaining your center and by maintaining the regularity of your breathing and a balanced sense of yourself in your surroundings.

For the teacher to be centered when the class is anxious, angry, confused, or scared is especially helpful. When one person in a group remains centered, distress is less contagious and the waves of distress settle more quickly.

Activity 18
Breathing to regain the center of the self

Note: This is a different and simpler version of Activity 17.

1. Let's stop for just a moment. Please sit up straight. Now take a few deep breaths. Breathe very deeply and slowly. Be aware of your breath coming in and going out. Breathe slowly and deeply. (*Pause*)

2. Now we can resume our activities. But note that whenever you find yourself being tight, or confused, or bothered, or blocked, you can stop for a moment and take a few deep breaths. Then keep breathing regularly—this will usually help you to become more balanced and to function more freely.

One teacher says—

"I sometimes have my fifth graders rediscover their whole selves, especially when I want them to be relaxed and free for doing something imaginative or having a discussion about themselves or their emotions. I find centering relaxes them. We all feel better and do better work. One time I led them through the steps of a centering activity and then asked them to say positive things to one another. They did a marvelous job. They were much freer and more open than they would have been without centering."

Activity 19
Rediscovering the whole self

1. Close your eyes and search for tension in any part of your body. When you find tension, use a tense-relax sequence to discharge that tension. (*For more specific suggestions, see Activity 1.*)

2. Repeat a mantra (*See Activity 15.*) to yourself until the word or phrase has neutralized your thoughts and relaxed your awareness.

3. When relaxed, start breathing more deeply. Imagine energy flowing into your body as you breathe in, and out as you breathe out.

4. Get in touch with some feelings that are important to your being. Perhaps focus on one of the following:
   —feelings of loving and being loved;
   —feelings of being strong and powerful;
   —feelings of being purposeful and wise.
   Allow these feelings to flow with your breath, through your body and your mind, bringing strength, healing, relaxation, and peace.

5. If you are with others, hold hands with some others and let the energy of your feelings flow through your hands, from you to your neighbor and from your neighbor to you. This reminds us how others can help vitalize and support our important emotions.

6. Break hands but maintain the sense of togetherness. Then slowly place yourself in the present. Open your eyes; study some of the vivid colors around you and the space around everything. Close your eyes again. Sense the floor securely holding you up. Open your eyes and gradually get yourself ready for your next activity.

Discovery takes place,
not when the mind is crowded
with knowledge,
but when knowledge is absent;
only then is there stillness and space,
and in this state
understanding or discovery
comes into being.

Krishnamurti

Activity 20
The listening activity

1. Please close your eyes and relax. Try a few deep breaths. (*Pause*)

2. Now do some listening. First I'd like you to hear all that you can that is outside this room. (*Pause a little longer.*)

3. Now let your ears pick up sounds that are inside this room. (*Pause*)

4. Now be very quiet and listen to the sound that is inside your head. (*Pause*)

5. Now listen to your whole self. Use the center of your body to hear with instead of your ears.

6. You can return to that sound within you whenever you want to feel more whole and relaxed. Your inner sound is comforting and always true to you. But now, slowly get yourself ready to come back to the group. Open your eyes whenever you are ready. Open them gently, easily.

Note: Fortunately or unfortunately, not everyone will hear his or her inner sound every time. You might tell students that the more quiet they are the more likely they are to hear themselves.

A thought before using Activity 21—

Some of our deepest feelings and thought fragments pop up in a dream form or are more comfortably related in a dream context. But we often have no one to tell our dreams to. Dreams stay muffled inside us when they would prefer to come out, be recognized, and be shared.

An awareness of our dreams is an awareness of an important part of ourselves. Understanding what a dream really means is not important, but if we are to be whole, greeting our dreams on some neutral ground is important.

Activity 21
The dream exchange

1. Think of a dream you have had recently. Or, recall a dream you have had more than once. Or, imagine a dream that you would like to have someday.

2. Sit with two persons you do not know too well—not your best friends—and take turns listening to one another's dreams. Don't try to understand or study the dreams you hear; just listen to the dreams your partners have had or would like to have someday.

Note: Afterwards, your class might have an open discussion of the feelings each participant experienced while sharing his or her dreams. Some of the questions you might discuss are the following: How many enjoyed the activity? Felt relieved to hear others' dreams? Would like to do it again sometime?

Also use the following activities to help the students center themselves—

—Have your students list their priorities and decide which are most important.
—Encourage the students to remind themselves that help and support are available and that one need not be vulnerable and alone.
—Invite the students to recollect their pasts, trying to sense the large movements and the trends.
—Have the students write self-contracts to help them accomplish chosen tasks and goals.
—Help the students decide if their current lives are too full and what, if anything, could be eliminated or deferred.
—Encourage discussions about feeling a part of nature. Ask: In what ways are we and animals the same? We and mountains? Is a mountain more or less important than a person? What love is between you and flowers?

Use the following questions to evaluate the success of the centering-the-self activities—

—Do you continue, even in distressing times, to breathe regularly and deeply, with a balanced sense of what is important?

—Do students who have experienced centering act more purposefully and consistently and less impulsively and immaturely?

—Has centering produced an increase in expressions of positive feelings, like affection, loyalty, and responsibility for oneself among the students?

—Do students report that they use centering to reduce temper flareups and perpetuation of conflicts?

—Does centering help you shift a group from a state of distress to one of balance and readiness for learning?

—Do students report that they like centering and that they use it out of school or have taught it to others?

6
Activities for giving the self messages

Giving oneself messages is the sending of imaginative or verbal messages to oneself to guide one's life.

Society is full of complicated, contradictory and not always kindly messages for us. Many of these we have absorbed unwittingly, especially when young. Some of these may confuse us, lead us to distrust and undermine ourselves. And we ourselves are usually not slow in noticing that other lives seem better, more successful, less confusing than ours. These many and varied messages can defeat and frustrate us if we allow them to penetrate our self-worth. Where and how do we learn to sort out which messages to accept and which to ignore? And where do we learn how to give ourselves the messages we decide are best for us?

This chapter considers activities for enabling us to give ourselves positive and helpful messages.

Activities for giving the self messages might be useful—

—when students give signs of feeling weak, inadequate, or bad about themselves;
—when a student shows a readiness to change;
—before a situation that has failure potential for students;
—to remind students regularly that they can help determine their own futures;
—when students need their confidence and strength repaired after a severe loss or punishment.

...our normal waking consciousness...
is but one special type of consciousness,
whilst all about it, parted from it
by the filmiest of screens, there lie
potential forms of consciousness entirely
different. We may go through life without
suspecting their existence, but apply the
requisite stimulus, and at a touch they are
there in all their completeness. ... No
account of the universe in its totality can be
final which leaves these other forms of
consciousness quite disregarded. How to
regard them is the question, for they are so
discontinuous with our ordinary
consciousness... at any rate, they forbid a
premature closing of our accounts with
reality.

William James

Activity 22
Sending general messages

Note: Read this activity to yourself and then put its steps into your own words.

1. Select a message for students to internalize. Have each student select his or her own message or provide a selection of messages, one of which might be selected for the entire group. Some sample messages are the following:

     Messages related to school work—
     —I will easily remember my multiplication table.
     —I will be curious about history.
     —I will remember that *i* usually comes before *e*.
     —I will find reading easy and enjoyable.
     More general messages—
     —I will relax when I am feeling nervous.
     —I will love myself.
     —I will be a fast runner.
     —I will take better care of myself.
     —I will be good looking to others.
     —I will not think in ways that make me nervous or scared.
     —I can do what I decide to do.
     —I am strong and wise.
     —I can control myself.
     —I will act responsibly.
     —I am a good person and a good friend.
     —I will think before I act.

2. For this activity, students must be relaxed and open. Use tension discharging, mind clearing, or repeating a mantra to prepare that situation. *(See Chapters 2, 3, 4.)*

3. While eyes are closed and while students are relaxed and centered, ask the students to repeat the selected message to themselves silently, slowly, and evenly.

4. Ask the students to imagine what their lives would be like if they believed the messages they selected. Say something similar to the following:

    If you really believed your message, if you were the kind of a person for whom that message was true, what kind of life would you lead? Imagine some things you would do. Imagine how others would treat you.

5. Or, ask the students to imagine themselves facing a specific situation.

    If you are using a whole-group message, select an appropriate situation for the students. For example, try,

    Imagine now that you are picking up your reading book. And imagine that you really believe that reading will be easy and enjoyable for you. In your mind, play through what would happen and how you would feel picking up the book, opening it, looking at it, and so on.

    If each student has a different message, ask the students to pick their own specific situations. Say something like the following:

    Imagine how tomorrow or any other day might be different if you fully believed your message. What is one thing that might happen? Pick a specific situation, and imagine where you are, what is in the scene, and who is there. Can you see it? Then, in your mind, play through the scene, being very aware of what would happen, how you would feel, what would happen next, and so on, as if you really believed your message.

6. Give students a period of silence in which to assimilate their messages. When most of the students have spontaneously opened their eyes, share reactions to the experiences or begin the next activity.

A thought about using Activity 22—

It's important to pick positive messages to give to yourself. Saying to yourself, "I will not reach for a cigarette when I feel the urge," gives you less power than saying, "I will relax and feel strong when I feel the urge to smoke." Similarly, "I will talk less compulsively" is a less effective self-message than "I will soothe my impulses and go slowly when I feel the need to speak." Whenever possible, state in your message what you *will choose to do* rather than what you will not do. Choosing to act in a positive way somehow makes listening to yourself easier.

Activity 23
The fantasy story

Note: Read this activity to yourself and then put it into your own words.

1. Select the message the students are going to internalize.
2. Ask the students to close their eyes and possibly to rest their heads on their arms.
3 Recount a fantasy story that concludes with individuals making decisions about their lives. The following is a sample story with indicated pauses for reading:

Imagine getting on a rocket ship that soars high into the sky, far, far away....And you enjoy the clouds, and the sunlight, and the view of the earth far below....You feel free, secure in your rocket ship, happy to be alone in the skies....You feel the lightness and the space all about....Imagine that you are a smart person, a very good thinker....You understand many things very easily...naturally.... And you fly in the rocket feeling your wisdom, your intelligence, and your goodness....Now you decide to take the rocket down, little by little, soaring up and dipping down as you like....And you are still feeling very wise, intelligent, good....Little by little, take the rocket down to earth....And as you do it, keep strong the feeling of being wise and good....When you are ready, land your rocket....And when you are feeling wise and good, open your rocket door and walk out....Keep feeling wise and good and walk home....Imagine being home and feeling wise and good....See what happens at home....Now imagine coming to school and feeling wise and good....Think of how things will be....When you feel secure and are happy that you are wise and good, open your eyes slowly, gradually settle back with us here in class, and let's hear about how you enjoyed your trip.

83

Activity 24
Side-stepping negative energy*

Note: Read this activity to yourself and then put it into your own words.

1. Have students discharge their tensions, perhaps using one of the first four activities in this book.

2. Have the students close their eyes. Tell the following story about Harriet:

   Harriet came home one day and her brother yelled at her for messing up his toys. The negative energy from her brother hit Harriet squarely and entered her mind and heart. She felt awful, angry at her brother, hurt by the negative energy he shot out at her.

   Elaborate the story as necessary, and then pause briefly so students can mull on the story.

3. Encourage the students to keep their eyes closed. Tell a story about Sidestepping Stella:

   Stella came home and her brother yelled at her for messing up his toys. But Stella told herself that, although her brother was full of negative energy and was throwing lots of it her way, she did not have to let the anger hit her. So she just stood there listening to her brother but sidestepping the energy he was throwing around, so that none of it entered her to mess her up. She said to herself, "My brother is very angry. But there's no reason why I must let that anger get into me." She let the negative energy fly past her like a warm breeze. Later, when her brother calmed down, they talked about that toy problem rather calmly.

   Elaborate if necessary and pause for private reflection.

4. While requesting that the students keep their eyes closed, ask them to imagine someone throwing negative energy their way:

   Now imagine that you are telling yourself that you will simply step aside and let the energy fly past you. Just because the other person needs to throw it in your direction, you need not let it enter your mind or heart. Imagine yourself saying that to yourself.

5. Ask students to open their eyes and discuss how they feel about the activity thus far. Then ask them for examples of how a person might use this idea of side-stepping anger. Finally, discuss how people in a disagreement can calmly look for alternative solutions to their problems after anger has been vented.

6. To give the students practice with this side-stepping skill, repeat step four. Then recommend that they repeat the activity themselves from time to time until they feel comfortable using it.

*Special thanks to Gay Hendricks and Russel Wills for the title of this activity.

One teacher says—

"I'm a high school history teacher. I have a few students every year with whom I have trouble. Sometimes I talk with them but the talk never seems to accomplish anything. The students slip back into their disruptive or self-defeating ways. But now, after a student and I agree that something should be different, I use a messaging procedure to help the student accept the change at a deeper than lip-service level. It really works wonders for some of the students."

Activity 25
Your own experimentation

Note: This page awaits your own experimentation to find an activity to calm and free student energies.

1 _____

_____

_____

_____

_____

_____

2 _____

_____

_____

_____

_____

3 _____

_____

_____

_____

_____

_____

One teacher's report—

Ingrid Brady is a third-grade teacher at an elementary school near Ames, Iowa. Ingrid exudes a love of teaching both in conversation and in professional behavior. Here is a report on how she teaches spelling:

"The teacher began class activities with some physical exercises apparently designed to stimulate a fun atmosphere and physically prepare and relax the kids. Students did stretching exercises while imagining that they were picking fruits from tall trees. The kids responded with tumultuous enjoyment, while Ingrid herself led them through each exercise. Her guidance was obvious but did not seem overwhelming. The pupils' attention was keenly drawn to the teacher's child-like behavior demonstrating how things were to be done.

"After exercises were completed in a matter of four or five minutes, students were asked to lie on the carpeted floor. They rested their heads comfortably on the soft carpet, and flute music began to pour out of two speakers strategically placed in the classroom. The piece was one of Herbie Mann's arrangements of 'Tangiers', Embryo Records SD 520. The kids seemed attentive and relaxed while Ingrid directed them to listen to the music. A short while later, she asked them to shift their attention from the music to their breathing and, without attempting to control it, simply to 'watch' it. After approximately six minutes, her soft voice brought them slowly out of their reveries, indicating that it was now time to resume activities.

"Seated in a semicircle on the soft carpet, teacher and pupils then began the joyous process of spelling roughly twenty words. Cards on which letters of the alphabet were written were distributed to each student. In the next half hour they spelled through each word by placing together the letters each student had received. As each word was sung out, pupils holding the appropriate letters would get up off the semicircle and stand together. It took roughly twelve minutes to go through all new words. It was evident that everyone enjoyed the exercise.

"Afterwards, everyone went back to a relaxed position on the carpet to listen to a portion of Antonio Vivaldi's 'Spring', from the Four Seasons composition. While pupils listened to the music, Ingrid intoned each one of the words to the cadence and rhythm of the music, giving the spelling, the meaning, and the words as she went."

A report from the *Newsletter* of the *Society for Suggestive Accelerative Learning and Teaching,* an organization that makes much use of relaxation and of suggestions telling students that they will learn comfortably and deeply. For information, write SALT, P. O. Box 815, Des Moines, Iowa 50306.

**Also use the following activities to help the students
give themselves messages—**

—Allow students to study things that interest them and in which
they can get genuinely involved.
—Use teaching strategies that provide students much success
and that allow them to correct errors without feeling
inadequate.
—Have students talk and write about the kinds of persons they
would like to be and how we can all help each other to
become what we choose to be.
—Create a classroom climate that is positive, warm, and
supportive.
—Notice students when they return from an absence, or are
wearing something attractive, or are doing something well, so
that each student feels important and worthy.

Use the following questions to evaluate the success of the messaging activities—

—Is there evidence that student behavior has changed in the direction of the positive messages that were used—that is, that the messages were in fact internalized?
—Do students report that the messaging process is helpful, that they use it out of school, or that they have taught it to others?
—Are students behaving more self-confidently and independently and less frequently asking for unnecessary help and advice since using the messaging activities?
—Do the messaging procedures help you more quickly repair specific troublesome times, as when a class or a student is discouraged?
—Do the messaging procedures help you support the growth decisions of particular students and more effectively help such students accomplish their goals?

7
Some questions we have heard and answers we have given

How do I justify time for such activities?

As with parents and supervisors, we would recommend that you tell students the truth as you know it. That is, that you tell, as simply as you can, why you think the activities are worth a try.
Especially consider these points:
—The procedures have a good chance of relaxing and settling people so that they can better think and plan and learn.
—The procedures, once taught to a group, can then be left to individuals to use if and when they find them to be useful.
—One does not have to be certain before experiencing a new procedure that it will be valuable. One reason we try new things is to determine if they are beneficial. If we didn't try new things, we would obviously miss out on many benefits.
Thus, we might say something like this to a class: "Let's try something new today. We'll try an activity that may help us to settle our minds and relax us, so we can learn better and live more easily together. We'll try this activity a few times and then we'll see if we like it."

At what ages can each of these activities be best done?

Actually, we don't know too much about that question. We would guess that your intuition, plus your trial experiences, will provide the best answer. Try a few activities that you feel might work. And be careful to adjust the language to fit your students' level of maturity, of course. It should be fairly obvious what, if anything, is working and what is not.

What do I say to parents or administrators who ask why I'm doing this?

Tell them why to the best of your ability. To clarify your own motivations, you might want to ask yourself some questions first: Do you simply want to try some new ideas to see if they can help you? Are you slightly bored with old routines and interested in adding something new to the classroom? Do you suspect that some students whom you have thus far been unable to help very much may be aided by these kinds of activities? Did students ask for them after you shared your reading of this book with them? Do you want to help students deal with stress in school and life? Are you interested in increasing learning in your classroom?

We recommend that you be honest about your motives to those who ask about them. A reasonable parent or administrator will understand a reasonable set of motives.

Those who are unreasonable, of course, may well require additional responses. Here, our initial approach is to ask for tolerance of an innovative approach until we can gather data to see what effects it has. Thus, we take an experimental stance, assert that we are taking that stance, watch to see what effects our innovations are having, and announce to others that we will discontinue any innovation that does not prove to be good for students.

Then, too, we as teachers are willing to stand on professional grounds and to talk about our responsibilities for our own work. We believe that teachers must make a myriad of decisions, decisions which cannot be programmed, and that we must be free to make those decisions if education is to be even minimally effective. You will have to judge to what extent you should make such an assertion, of course, but we often find that it clarifies our roles to those who have lost sight of what a good teacher must do.

Don't inner processes need to be connected to outer events?

Yes, but that perspective is relatively well developed nowadays. It is the other part, the awareness and management of inner processes, that our culture by and large has neglected.

Even psychologists and psychiatrists often attempt to solve our inner problems by looking at them from the outside, asking what caused them or what effects they are having on our surroundings. As our inner reality gets objectified in that way, we probably become less and less respectful of that reality, and more and more alienated from ourselves. And we may despair—Who will ever understand what I am? Especially when I cannot find words to talk about it?

To get a hold on a problem that this relative neglect of our inner processes has been causing us, consider the high school student who finds himself feeling vaguely discontented. Since he has been acculturated to look outwards, his first impulse will probably be to seek outside causes for his malaise. He'll ask himself, "What out there is making me feel this way?" And since causes for human conditions are rarely if ever simple, our young man will rarely if ever answer his question accurately. But having no other question to ask, he will answer the question as best he can, which means inaccurately. He might blame his friends, or the school faculty, or his family, or the state of the world. He might even communicate that blame to the parties concerned, who will probably react by becoming distressed themselves and perhaps by distressing him more in return. Thus, not only will he have failed to approach his situation comprehensively, but he will have made it worse.

He would do better to get in touch with the whole of his discontent and consider what aspects of it might be unrelated to his surroundings. If he has skills to deal with what he found inside himself, he might well escape his discontent more quickly and comfortably.

Don't teachers have enough trouble now, without adding all this new stuff?

Yes and no. Teachers do have a hard enough job, but we believe that these activities make the job more satisfying and more effective, not harder and more complicated. We doubt that most people will know much of what is involved in these activities by simply reading through the book. We believe the activities have to be experienced, by you and your students, before they can be fairly known.

Do your ideas have anything to do with TM?

TM, or Transcendental Meditation, is but one of the many approaches to internal processes. Although we have learned from the TM experience, and we are particularly grateful for their efforts in bringing meditation to the attention of many people in the West, the procedures in this book are based on a more varied body of thought and experience. Our base not only includes schools of meditation other than TM but also findings from mental health and educational psychology and, especially, our own experiences in teaching others to relax and to better manage their whole energies.

Are there some situations in which these activities will not work?

They will not work if they are used punitively or manipulatively or if the atmosphere in which they are used is punitive or manipulative.

What about frequency of use?

We would not recommend using more than one activity a day as a usual procedure. And we do not recommend that you teach students more than one new activity a week. It is often wise, we feel, to try one activity two or three times the first week you introduce it. After that minimum test, decide whether or not it should be added to your ongoing repertoire of classroom strategies.

Do any hazards come with these procedures?

Some students, such as those who have serious difficulty separating fantasy and reality, for example, may find some of the fantasy activities to be unpleasant experiences. However, we have no reason to believe that these students will be harmed by them, especially if an activity is not forced upon them but rather offered as a group experience, enabling each individual to make more or less of it as he or she wishes.

But not enough evidence exists to be certain that absolutely no hazards exist. Our recommendation would be that a watch be kept for frustrations, angers, fears, or other indications that a student is being served badly just as you would keep watch over activities as common as the reading of a sad story or the organizing of teams to compete in a spelling bee. We believe such students should be protected, even when it means temporarily depriving the rest of the group of a meaningful experience.

In general, we know of no potential problems that are serious enough to require more than an everyday level of teacher vigilance.

How can I evaluate the effectiveness of the activities?

It depends on the kind of information that is necessary. If you want to relay this information to someone whose intuition and empathy are alive, have that person observe you and your students during the activities. A fairly complete evaluation is possible if you supplement such observations with subjective reports from you and your students, saying how the procedures seemed to affect each of you.

If you want to describe the effectiveness of the activities to persons who prefer less subjective data, a good plan is to turn some of the evaluation questions listed in each section of the book into observation schemes and then to report those observations. For example, you might turn the evaluation question "Does learning improve?" into an observation of test scores before and after the use of the procedures.

Consider, also, making these before-and-after observations:
—Count absences. Simply check to see if there is a trend in the number of absences. If possible, sort out those absences attributable to accidents and serious illnesses. If there are fewer absences, consider it evidence that something good has been going on.
—Count referrals to the principal's office. Or keep count of the number of punishments or scoldings you administer each day.
—Count the number of students in class before and after hours. If students voluntarily come earlier and stay later it's probably a good sign of effectiveness.
—Make a good-day survey. On some regular basis, ask students leaving class to check a rating scale, from one to ten, that asks "How good was your day today?"
—Try a simple phone or mail survey of a sample of the parents, asking how often students speak about their school days positively, not at all, or negatively.
—Obtain a test that measures mental health or self-concept. Don't expect to improve the mean scores on such a test, for that may be too much to expect from any classroom

experiment, but hope that over time you can reduce the number of persons with low scores.

—Develop a rating scale for such items as cooperation, open-mindedness, flexibility, politeness. Ask other teachers, parents, and the students themselves to rate these items on a before and after basis.

Are these activities really worth the time they will take away from academic learning?

That question makes us wonder about the perceptions people have about schooling. We see the graduates of our schools as taking with them into adult life precious little of the academic learning that was heaped upon them. We wonder how much would be lost if even half of the time spent in school was devoted to non-academic growth. Half of precious little is not very much.

But, more directly, the evidence is that time used in these activities can produce a net increase in learning. The activities seem to be able to make available to students more of their intelligence and creativity and/or to remove some of their blocks to cognitive functioning. But you will have to determine if these results apply to your students in your situation. As yet, insufficient evidence exists for us to feel secure in making generalizations.

By the way, some teachers find no evidence that the procedures help with learning, but neither do they find that they reduce learning. They feel that students somehow learn as much as they ever did, even after part of the class time is reserved for inner management activities. The question then is whether or not the activities are justified in terms of improved classroom climate, ease in teaching, or non-academic student growth.

How do we know how slowly or quickly to go with these procedures?

That's always a problem. When working with a group, there is always the reality that what is too fast for some will be too slow for others. With the very personal activities of this book, this is a special problem. But here are some hints about pacing:
—Whenever possible, experience the activities yourself several times before you use them on others. That will give you a "feel" for the activities.
—Avoid calling out unnecessary directions when students have their eyes closed and are into themselves, for that is apt to jolt some from their thoughts. Rather, watch students' breathing and eyes. Deep and regular breathing is a sign that students have reached a level of relaxation. Eyes opening indicate that it will soon be time for the next step.
—Sample the progress of a group by whispering to one or two students "Are you ready for the next step yet?"
—Tell students in advance that you want them to raise their hands whenever they are ready for the next step.

What do you mean when you say that these activities can help students deal with stress?

We see stress as a serious problem in our time. More and more persons, young and old, seem to be suffering too much emotional or mental strain, as if life is too complicated, unstable, or distressing for them.

A little stress can, of course, be exciting. But a lot of stress or unresolved stress can soon lead to hyperactivity and a loss of direction. If stress continues, we are apt to feel confused and lose our abilities to concentrate. Not far behind are expressions of exhaustion and frustrations, and a situation in which depression or violence can grow.

Activities such as those in this book tend to separate us from the tensions in the air. They help us stay connected to our best instincts, our most healthy motives, and our wisest perspectives. They help us to discharge safely the pressures that build when we hear such sentences as "You must stay on top of all the pressures around you," "Whether you like it or not ...," "You are not excellent because...," "It's hopeless to...." They help us rather to see the truth in such sentences as "We do not have to respond to every pressure from our environment," "We have integrity and we can choose," "We can do better," and "We all are persons with power, wisdom, and goodness."

In short, we see possibilities that procedures like ours can help students—and ourselves too—to change pressures that we experience only as excessive noise into motives that power our best intentions and potentials.

How do I know when to stop repeating a mantra?
Will I hear what's going on around me?
Can I do this by myself, anyplace, any time?

Fifteen to twenty minutes is the commonly recommended time span for repeating a mantra. It's useful to keep a clock nearby and to glance at the time every once in a while. If twenty minutes have passed, you might want to stop and turn to other matters. You will find, by the way, that when you really get the knack of repeating your mantra, time will zip along magically. Before you know it, the clock will have jumped ahead and you will be relaxed.

Will you hear what's going on around you? You certainly will. Repeating the mantra does not clog hearing at all. You do not fall asleep. You will be able to hear people, the telephone, doors opening, and so on, and if something comes up that you would rather attend to, you can simply discontinue the mantra, open your eyes, and do what you wish.

Can you repeat a mantra any place? Yes, although it's usually wise to do this where interruptions are least likely to occur. Some people meditate successfully on a train or bus, sitting in a waiting room, in a room with others after asking not to be disturbed, or in a library.

Can I use these procedures to control a misbehaving student?

It depends. If the relationship between you and the student is not already somewhat positive, it seems to us unlikely that the student will give these activities a good enough try. A certain minimum amount of student willingness and time and effort is required to show results.

On the other hand, if you have students (or whole groups) who wish to control their own disruptive impulses and simply are not able to do so, there is a very good chance that these activities will be helpful.

Many misbehaving students, of course, need to receive messages of their own sanity and self-worth. Try getting such students to talk out their frustrations and negative feelings. Listen without becoming tense or excited. Then help the students to relax with a soothing mantra. Also help them discharge physical tensions by giving them room to move around and exercise. When they are relaxed, tell them that they are worthwhile and that they should take care of themselves. Later, react to types of behavior that show strength and competence and self-acceptance. Do not use your energy to support negative thoughts or types of behavior.

What do I do if the class is generally noncooperative?

It is important that you yourself become centered and do not add to a bad atmosphere with impulsive or desperate kinds of behavior.

If you are upset and being thrown off center by disruptive types of behavior, so are the students. Talk about the situation and try to agree to share the responsibility for a constructive atmosphere. This includes having other students who are being disturbed communicate their feelings evenly and without hostility to those who are doing the disturbing.

Of course, it is wise to check to see if elements of your class curriculum have contributed to student resistance. Is there plenty of respect and acceptance in the room? Is there little frustration and failure? Is there variety and even delight on occasion? Are there patterns that nourish the egos of the students?

When you have established positive patterns, inner management activities become possible and will work to further strengthen the atmosphere in the classroom.

Can one find inner peace in an insane society?

Maybe and maybe not. But if we can learn to manage our inner processes, that will at least help us to avoid contributing to the insanities of society.

Can these activities be as cut and dried as your formulas seem to make them?

The activities even seem dry to us when we read back over them. The descriptions can seem too pat, inflexible, and standard as they sit there in cold type. To make it all real, we must use our own imaginations and envision active humans experiencing the activities. We would urge you to do that, too.

Use our suggestions as guides. Experiment. Change our sequences if your experiences or intuitions suggest it. Feel free to omit or add elements, or to take elements from different activities and create new ones. Certainly change the language and elaborate on the steps so that the students understand and accept the directions.

Most importantly, orient yourself as fully as you can to the humans with whom you deal and to your own rich self. Keep tuned into life. And remember that we are talking about human transactions and that all such transactions thrive on empathy, warmth, and honesty.

In short, we hope that you will use our guidelines creatively and responsively, incorporate our suggestions into your own perceptions, and use them in a way that suits your style and your situation. Making the suggestions relevant and alive is, in fact, the only way to insure that the activities will have their best chance of being helpful to you.

*Should I insist that reluctant students
do these activities?*

We would say not. Motivate the group the best you know how;
then let students who remain resistant opt out and do something
else that does not disturb the rest of the group. If the
procedures you use turn out to be effective and if other students
profit from them, many reluctant students will later join in. And
if they don't? Nothing much is lost, and a demonstration of your
respect for individual differences and integrity is gained.
Resistant students, after all, will almost certainly gain nothing
from the activities they resist but are compelled to do. Teaching
is hard enough without asking yourself to drag along all students
through all experiences.

*Isn't inner contemplation an escape from the hard
questions of social reality? If we spend our time
contemplating, who will work at the real causes
of problems?*

It isn't either-or. There is no reason why we cannot work at
correcting social ills while we also relax our tensions and center
our awareness. Activities such as the ones in this book can be
expected to make us more effective at whatever we do, whether
we concentrate on social reform or private growth. These
procedures will not only energize our best motives but will also
help us to cooperate with each other, face opponents without
unduly inflaming their resistances, and recognize and avoid
diversionary battles.

　　There is, in fact, reason to conclude that our old efforts at
achieving social reform do not work very well. If we are to
escape the circles in which the world has been turning, we may
need new perspectives. If so, the activities we are
recommending might be valuable indeed.

Since doing activities like these is not my style,
would you recommend that I try them anyhow?

It depends on how much it's not your style. If you are simply
unfamiliar with procedures like these and somewhat at a loss as
to how to begin or what to expect if you do begin, we would
encourage you to try some of the activities. We know some
teachers who worked through their unfamiliarity, inertia, or
personal reluctance, tried the procedures, and were delighted
with the results.

But if you are genuinely uncomfortable, it's probably best to
skip these activities. Not every teacher has to do everything.
Leave these procedures to teachers who can learn to be
comfortable with them. It's best, we think, for each of us to do
what he or she does best and enjoys.

If these activities are not your style and yet you perceive that
your students might profit from them, you might pass this book
along to someone else who can work with your students and
help them with inner management skills. In that way, your
students' needs are met while you are not forced to operate in a
style uncomfortable to you. That's one of the beauties of team
teaching.

Why can't schools get along in the future
without these activities?

We'll use vitamins as an analogy. Sometimes, a person can get
along for years without the need for supplemental vitamins.
Then his or her body changes, or eating patterns change, or the
availability of nutritious food changes, and as a result, the
person either takes vitamins or suffers some deficiency. We
believe something like that has happened to our culture. Times
have changed in ways that make the activities we outline in this
book helpful to many people. Similarly, times may change again
and make them unnecessary. But, in the meantime, we would
recommend that you consider trying them and seeing if they in
fact do serve you and your students in some productive way.

*Aren't these activities religious and spiritual
in nature, and shouldn't they therefore be excluded
from schools?*

No. These activities train skills. Arithmetic teaches us skills
useful for calculating. These activities teach us skills useful for
constructively managing our energies.

*Why are so many people interested
in self-awareness, meditation, new religions,
and things like that these days?*

It's hard to account for swings in the public's interests, and it
may be presumptuous to believe that we will ever understand
ourselves well enough to do that, but we can speculate a bit.

Our speculation would begin with the observation that
more people nowadays seem at least vaguely apprehensive,
unsettled, insecure, or fearful. This might be a result of all the
changes that are taking place in society. Many people view
recent history as too much, too uncontrolled, too fast. The fears
we observe might also be connected to the increasing evidence
that the world's population will soon exceed the world's
resources. Or, the fears might be connected to suspicions that
our society, with all its technological brilliance, is somehow
off-base and will almost certainly be inadequate for the good-life
goals it advertises. Whatever the source of our fears, we are
increasingly an apprehensive people.

Now, one might ask, what does an apprehensive person do
nowadays? Our speculation sees this sequence: A person senses
discontent. The person does not see anything he or she can do
to influence the *source* of the discontent, which seems to be
someplace out there in society. So the person seeks to ease the
discontent by learning how to relax or by learning how to live
more comfortably in the society as it is. This brings him or her to

self-awareness topics and self-help procedures, including meditation and new religions.

From a somewhat different perspective, we might say that many people, unable to get security from the society in which they live, quite naturally seek more private places to anchor and secure their beings, places discussed less by scientists and politicians and more by philosophers, artists, psychologists, and mystics.

To speculate further, we note one other trend that could connect to the general increases in apprehension that we perceive. This trend deals with a preparation for the worst, such as a preparation for a very violent event. How does one get ready for violence? Partly by becoming accustomed to it, such as by choosing to experience violent stories and sports, so that any future violent event is less shocking if and when it comes. And partly by learning to take a passive, flow-with-it view of life, so that one does not judge what comes and so that even violence is less likely to be experienced as a negative event. We see some people doing each of those things. Perhaps some are doing both.

We are definitely of the opinion that these trends, if they are in some way connected to our general apprehension, are not connected consciously and deliberately. Someone or some group did not sit down and decide that this or that should occur. It is rather a matter of changes coming together for reasons we do not understand, just as we do not understand how salmon connect spawning to certain freshwaters or how the sight of a forgotten friend's face connects to his or her name in our memories. Although we know that these things happen, we often do not know how or why.

We may be all wrong about this. To be sure, it is all speculation. It is not speculative, however, to say that more people nowadays are drawn to self-awareness topics and self-help procedures and that educators will probably fill a real need if they provide assistance in these areas. Our preference, of course, is for assistance that does not merely divert, alleviate, or deaden anxieties, as alcohol and drugs do. Our preference is for assistance that leads individuals to strength, balance, and deep awareness, enabling them to shape their worlds more creatively.

108

8
An occasion to reassess one's teaching

Students squeeze down their energies or distort their selves for reasons, of course, and those reasons can often be traced to non-nurturing environments. When our healthy energies have no place to flow, those energies tend to dry up or shift into less healthy streams. It's our way of reducing frustrations.

A problem arises then for teachers who use the activities in this book to free up more of the essence of being a student: What are students to do with those new energies? If the curriculum is stifling, if there is no room for students to be themselves, if students are treated as *objects* upon which the school-institutions work rather than as *persons* who are themselves sources of creative energy, we would expect those new-found energies to twist and strain and eventually shut down again. Therefore, teachers using these activities might take some time to reassess their curricula by asking themselves the following questions:

Do students have sufficient choices to make? Can they, for example, sometimes choose in which order to do things, how much they are to do, how quickly they are to do certain things, how carefully they should do them, or even *what* they are to do? Choices must be kept on the right side of confusion, but even very young children can make some choices.

Are students treated as if they can understand and make judgments? Are they, for example, given sufficient explanations for rules, allowed to shape rules, and helped to learn how to share in rule enforcement?

Are there chances for students to get recognition, if they need it? And friendship or affection, if either of these is a need? And opportunities to talk through their wonderments and problems with others?

Is there a sufficient variety of activities so that students can meet their needs to move, talk, be thoughtful, take initiative, show weakness, and express the vital parts of themselves?

Those questions are meant only to be suggestive. We all tend to get confused from time to time and it is useful, we find, to stop and look about once in a while to get our bearings. One occasion for teachers to do this is in conjunction with the use of this book's activities. Especially if you employ some of the activities yourself so your own energies are flowing more richly and comfortably, you and the students together may be in a good position to cooperate and shift the curriculum closer to your ideals.

This is not the place for a complete discussion of curriculum alternatives, but here are notes about three of our favorite ideas.

Learning support groups

The main idea

The teacher divides the class into groups of four and calls them "support groups," announcing that those groups will remain together more or less permanently and will serve as one of the main organizing elements of the class.

What are learning support groups supposed to do?

Learning support groups provide an atmosphere in which students help each other understand things, point out one another's mistakes, and share their thoughts, ideas, feelings, and concerns. They also serve as a structure for small group discussions when they are needed, for such administrative tasks as collecting money and taking attendance, and for evaluation discussions of the class or of individual work.

Why use learning support groups?

—This curriculum alternative provides students with places to share comfortably their stories, their ideas, and their problems.

—Since the teacher does not have time to answer all questions and explain everything that students do not understand, the support group is a place to get help.
—Corrections that teachers make on papers are often not understood. In none-test situations, the support group may help each member to understand and correct errors or weaknesses in his or her work before it is presented to the teacher. Such cooperation is particularly effective in improving learning in creative writing, foreign language exercises, and mathematics.
—Students learn better when they have to explain, discuss, and teach each other what they have learned.
—Although these are not the only groups students will work in (pairs within support groups are sometimes a more natural work group, and various other and more temporary groups are recommended for other purposes), learning support groups provide each student with a home base in school, a source of new friends, and a base of security. This can be very valuable, especially for students who do not have many friends or who do not have a secure or warm family at home. For the teacher, the groups provide an organizational structure that can be called on for many purposes at any time.

Two important don'ts for learning support group interaction:

1. No put downs
   Don't put others down. Don't call names. Don't ask questions meant to show another person's ignorance.
2. No sponging
   Don't do another person's work. Don't have others do your work.

Four key do's:

1. Use the rule of encouragement
   Talk about—discuss—draw out—*focus on what is good.*
2. Use the rule of drawing out
   Ask questions to help you understand the other person and

his or her thoughts. Ask about "how." Ask about "why." Ask for explanations. Ask for details. Ask for reasons. Ask for examples. But ask in a kindly, no-put-down tone.
3. Use the rule of reflection
Often people repeat themselves and feel badly because they think they have not been heard or understood. Often, misunderstandings and conflicts arise because people have not understood each other. So show you understand. Show this by repeating back to the person the essense of what he or she said. You might start in one of the following ways, "I hear you saying . . . ." "Do you mean . . . ." "As I understand it, you mean . . . ." Before disagreeing, be sure you show the other person that you understand his or her statement. This will avoid misunderstandings, hurt feelings, anger, and waste of time.
4. Use the rule of explanation
When someone does not understand something, he or she may feel confused, inadequate, and tense. Fast talking, anger, or shouting makes it harder for him or her to understand. When explaining something—
—Start with what the other person understands.
—Say one thing at a time in a slow, calm, and clear voice.
—Check to see that the other person understands what you have said by having him or her repeat your statement and explain it before going on to the next step.
—Review frequently by summarizing the steps of your statement. Then make sure the other person understands the summary.

Long-range results of the learning support group:

Clarity
Understanding
Empathy
Peace
Morale
Friendship
Cooperation
Learning
Wisdom

In general

The key element of learning support groups is *stability*. In a support group situation, students do not have to worry about talking with new people each day, and they have time to work out healthy relationships. Also, the teacher has a ready-made small group structure on which to call. We find that most groups can remain together for several months but that others are best reorganized sooner if they can't easily work together. We also find that best friends sometimes interfere with productive group work, so we often place them in different groups. But experiment a bit, accept some failure as a likely price of innovation, and see what works best in your situation.

Group planning sessions

The main idea

Today's students seem to have a special need to see themselves as respected persons and as partly responsible for their environments. One way to insure that they sense that respect and have room to learn responsibility is to formalize the existence of group planning sessions. From time to time, the class should sit together as a group to talk through problems or to think openly about issues, both subject matter issues and general issues.

How might group planning be used?

—To get a general assessment of how things have been going and to open possibilities for constructive change, periodically ask the group how well the class has been doing. (Learning support groups might discuss this issue before the large group meeting.)
—Occasionally, start a new unit of study by doing some planning with the group. Perhaps fill up the chalkboard with

answers to these questions: What are some things you know about this topic? What are some things you do not know? How might we proceed to study it further?

—Use brainstorming to explore what might be done about a class problem, such as persistent boredom, persistent tardiness, lost supplies, disinterested class members, teasing on the playground.

—Use special meetings for special occasions, such as planning a party or making a class decision.

—Conduct special meetings to handle topics suggested by one or more learning support groups. This allows the groups to initiate class discussion topics and thus helps bring hidden feelings to the surface and eliminate problems associated with them.

Suggestions for planning meetings:

—Listen to everyone. Do not put down anyone.

—Have private meetings with someone who is disruptive or talks too much to help him or her understand the impact of those types of behavior on others.

—Brainstorm alternatives to problems and then go back and evaluate the alternatives. During the evaluation, consider both what you *think* and what you *feel* about each alternative.

—Include plenty of quiet times, pauses for thinking, and temporary shelving of issues.

—Employ the frequent use of pairs or other small group discussions in the midst of large group meetings, especially when many students have the need to talk or when a sensitive topic makes small group talk easier than large group talk. After a break for small group discussions, resume large group discussion. (It is usually not necessary, or advisable, to have all small groups bother to report what they discussed.)

—Let the group decide some issues while at other times accept only advice. When you choose not to give over responsibility to the group to make a decision, explain the reason for that choice: that you prefer to keep control over this, the law requires it, the school policy dictates it.

—Support the chairing of group meetings by the teacher or by students on a rotating basis.
—Conduct a brief evaluation of a group planning session at the end. How did we do? What did we learn? How might we do better next time? Group planning meetings are meant to be serious and important cooperative experiences; we want students to keep learning how to do better with them.

Learning projects

The main idea

Support groups and group planning meetings are cooperative experiences from which students learn something about sharing intelligence and democratic decision-making. But students also need to learn more about individual self-discipline and how learning fits into the whole of life. Project work is a valuable tool for these purposes.

A project to us is essentially a small or large task undertaken by a student—or sometimes two or three students working together—during which students have space to exercise self-discipline and creativity. Younger students typically accept smaller projects: taking turns straightening the desks or drawing pictures to send to grandparents. Older students tackle larger projects: running a school store or writing learning packets for next year's classes.

We find that the key distinction between a project's being a mere activity time and a project's being a learning experience is *disciplined reflection*.

How can the teacher encourage disciplined reflection?

—Ask students to evaluate their work each time they work on their projects. Ask them questions like: How well did you do today? How could you have done better? What did you learn?
—Ask students to plan ahead, when that is appropriate, by asking: Have you a goal in mind? Do you wish to explore

without a goal? What materials or assistance do you need? How will you go about getting what you need?

—Focus student attention on the processes they use by asking: What feelings came up for you? What adjustments did you make? Did you have any difficulties with self-discipline or cooperation with others? How did you handle difficulties? How could you do better next time? What did you learn about yourself?

—Focus student attention on the subject matter outcomes by asking: What knowledge did you develop? What skills did you improve? How might those be useful in the future? Where might you go from here?

What kinds of projects could you consider?

Academic Projects: Learn something from Chapter 4.... Make a scale drawing of....Create a new example of....Teach each other the materials on pages....Find your own way to learn....

Integrated Projects (not narrowly based on subject matter): Grow plants or help to grow a garden....Make a mural....Write and produce a play for the younger students....Produce a small newspaper....Invent something new for the class.

Field Projects (out of the classroom): Make a traffic survey around the school....Take a poll to see what others know about or feel about a specific matter....Interview some senior citizen about the past....Observe other people and things for two hours in a factory, police station, supermarket, or any other interesting place....Construct a shed for the playground equipment.

Service Projects (to exercise citizenship): Donate time to help in a hospital, city hall, or service organization....Start a new service to the community....Help some senior citizens with shopping or cleaning....Work with younger children in some way....Clean up and improve parks.

Perhaps you will want to brainstorm other projects with groups of students, teachers, and parents and prepare a master list of project options for all teachers.

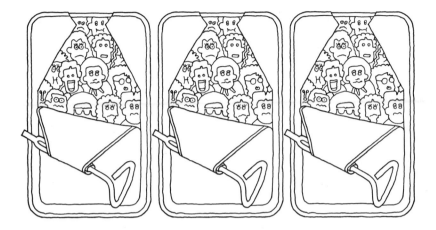

Do you know what intelligence is?
It is the capacity, surely, to think freely,
without fear, without a formula,
so that you begin to discover for yourself
· what is real, what is true;
but if you are frightened
you will never be intelligent.

Krischnamurti

9
Applications to counseling

The activities in this book can serve an individual student as well as a group. Several activities are especially useful for students in distress. We have taught some of the relaxation exercises to students who suffered extreme anxiety. We have taught some of the mind-clearing activities to students who complained about confusion and over-stimulation. The centering activities have helped us with students who found themselves lost in too many pressures. Similarly effective have been those activities meant to assist a person in giving and receiving self-messages.

The various sections in this book point to the intended purpose of the activities, and although the sectioning is somewhat arbitrary and the purposes overlap, you can get a sense of what each activity can do from those section discussions.

But, as we have said before, the only way to get a reasonably complete sense of any of the activities is to try them, preferably on yourself first. We would recommend that a counselor pick a few activities that seem most likely to be useful, try them, make notes about what each seems to do, and then keep those notes handy so an activity can be called upon when an appropriate situation arises.

The activities can be taught to individuals for their own use at home and they can be used in the counseling session itself. In fact, we have found that it is best to first lead a person through an activity if we expect the person to use it later. Few persons who do not experience an activity that way are likely to employ it on their own.

Finally, note that the activities can often serve to teach something important to a person suffering life's problems. We typically employ the activities not only for the purposes discussed in this book, but also to open up new ways of looking at life and of managing it.

As one small example, consider the following transcript from a counseling session involving Saville and a woman teacher, whom we call Benitta. Benitta was having great difficulty knowing what to do with some energies within her that felt very frightening. She was alternatively drawn to and frightened away from an urge to let those energies flow.

B: "I don't want to block myself. I want to be able to fully experience what I am feeling, yet not be overcome by it. I don't want to stiffen or turn away from my feelings. I am afraid that my inclination to repress and deny is too strong."

S: "But you seem to be repressing more. I think it's important not to confuse intensifying a feeling with letting it be. If you are going to the dentist you don't have to be thinking about the fear and then putting it down. You can just think about it. And that's fine."

B: "Are you saying that not thinking about it is not necessarily repressing it? It's just not thinking about it?"

S: "Yes. And repressing it is doing two things at the same time—bringing it to awareness and pushing it down at the same time."

B: "When I'm feeling anxious and I don't want to block the feeling, when I don't want to deny it or bury it but instead I want to live through it, and I do want to feel less anxious, what should I do?"

S: "There are several things you can do. One, you can just maintain your breath. Then you know you are not blocking. You can let the thoughts come and let them go. That's a mind-clearing kind of thing. You know, just let thoughts or sensations flow through without heavily attending to them. You can even increase a flow by saying a mantra.

"Suppose you are feeling anxious and it isn't a time when you want to cope with the anxiety or turn it into problem solving. But you don't want to repress it either. You don't want to tighten up against it. You can lie down then and say the word *sunshine* in your head. And if the anxious thoughts come, you can let them come and then just go back to saying *sunshine*. As soon as you are aware that you are not saying *sunshine*, begin saying it again.

"Now saying *sunshine* will break up the contagion of anxiousness, and now the anxious thoughts will come up. You won't be able to keep them down, but you'll feel the anxiety momentarily and then you'll be off into your mantra again until you relax. And then you can pick up on where you want to go.

"If anxiety is heavier and you can't even say *sunshine* because the other thoughts are coming in continuously, again you can just maintain your breath and let them come, and face the pain of them. You'll find that they won't stay at an unbearable level for more than a minute or two. Or you can use a mantra from the source of the anxiety. Suppose you are anxious about your friend Amy—you can use *Amy* as a mantra. Using her name will block some of the contagion of anxiety. And yet the anxious feelings about her will be able to come up and dissipate, without going into an elaborate, circular, guilty kind of thing.

"While you are here you can think of something—let's say an intermediate anxiety—and use a mantra just to see how it works. Not a high anxiety, because you probably don't want to go into something with high anxiety right now."

B: "I have trouble with that because sometimes one thing will go quickly all the way from low anxiety to high anxiety, like money."

S: "Well, let's try money because you clearly have some anxiety about it but I don't get the sense that it is overwhelming to you right at this time."

After this session, Benitta wrote: "I relaxed at this point and repeated *money* over and over again. At first my anxiety increased. When I tried it again, however, I found that before long the word lost its meaning. It was like repeating a nonsense syllable repeatedly. And so, it worked."

At another tense moment, Benitta used a deep breathing activity to ease the pressure. She later relayed to Saville the following anecdote: "A week ago Sunday night at Amy's, I felt enormous pressure and frustration, quickly turned to anger. I felt explosive, like I wanted to throw things through the walls. I was physically distraught, anxious, overwhelmed. Finally, I decided to sit and breathe deeply, though doing that was very difficult. I wanted to be up and moving about, smashing things. But I found that as I breathed deeply, the pressure eased up a bit and I did not feel so compelled to throw things."

In responding to Benitta's story, Saville noted: "When you breathe deeply you are affirming your total self, including that part of you that values what you might be destroying. If you breathe deeply, you can't easily repress part of you. So you are feeling the anger but you are also feeling your positive values, which brings you into balance. This is so different from the solution in which you say, 'Well, this anger is destructive. I'll repress my breathing so I won't have to feel it'. And then, instead of being wholly activated, which can lead to a balanced solution, a problem-solving solution, you become wholly inactivated, which leads to a death-like solution, a non-being solution."

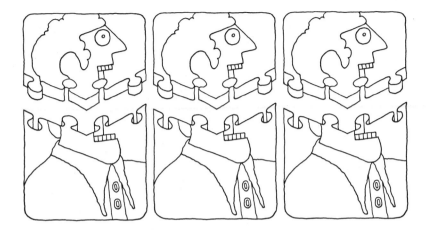

Vision comes when I'm alone
abandoned to imagination.

10
About resources

Where do all these activities come from? By and large, we have no idea. Most have existed for a long time and are simply being drawn into modern life because, we presume, of some current human need. It would be fair to characterize most of the book's activities as essentially our versions of older wisdom and practice.

The list below provides some guides to those who would study further. Five publications that were especially helpful as we prepared this book were the following:

Yoga for All Ages by Rachel Carr
Meta-Calisthenics by Lowell Miller
The Psychology of Consciousness by Robert Ornstein
Wake the Dragon by Saville Sax and Sandra Hollander
The Centering Book by Gay Hendricks and Russel Wills

Mostly we thank all those teachers, group leaders, and parents who experimented with activities and told us what worked and what didn't work. They helped turn our original set of ideas into the more refined selection that we present to you here.

But this is not the final selection, to be sure. We keep finding new activities and new ways to connect parts of old activities together, and we hope you will do that too. In that regard, we invite you to share your experiences with us. If ever a future edition of this book is needed, it would be good to have things you learned to add to it.

Contact us also if you would like a workshop for your group. Your group may be interested in experiencing some of the activities of this book, or some of the newer ones, or your group may wish to discuss the applicability of all of this to your particular situation. Contact us at Southern Illinois University, Edwardsville, IL 62026.

M.H./S.S.

Bibliography

Ajaya, Swami, ed. *Psychology East and West*. Glenview,
Ill.: Himalayan Institute, 1976.

Anderson, Marianne S., and Savary, Louis. *Passages: A
Guide for Pilgrims of the Mind*. New York: Harper &
Row, 1973.

Ballentine, R., ed. *Theory & Practice of Meditation*.
Glenview, Ill.: Himalayan Institute, 1975.

Benson, Herbert. *The Relaxation Response*. New York:
William Morrow & Company, Inc., 1975.

Bloomfield, Harold H.; Cain, Michael Peter; Jaffe,
Dennis T.; and Kory, Robert B.. *TM*. New York:
Dell, 1976.

Brooks, Charles. *Sensory Awareness*. New York:
Viking Press, 1974.

Campbell, Colin. "Transcendence Is As American As
Ralph Waldo Emerson." *Psychology Today*. Vol. 7,
No. 11:37-38, April 1974.

Carr, Rachel. *Yoga for All Ages*. New York: Simon and
Schuster, 1972.

Castillo, Gloria A. *Left-Handed Teaching*. New York:
Praeger Publishers, 1974.

Clynes, Manfred. *Sentics: The Touch of Emotions*. New
York: Doubleday, 1977.

DeMille, Richard. *Put Your Mother on the Ceiling*. New
York: The Viking Press, 1973.

Denniston, Denise, and McWilliams, Peter. *The TM Book*.
New York: Warner Books, 1976.

Diskin, Eva. *Yoga for Children*. New York: Warner Books, 1976.

Ferguson, Phillip C. "Transcendental Meditation and Its
Potential Application in the Field of Special Education."
The Journal of Special Education. 10:211-220, Summer 1976.

Foundation, Lama. *Be Here Now*. Crown, 1971.

Goleman, Daniel. "Meditation Helps Break the Stress
Spiral." *Psychology Today*. pp. 82-86, 93, February 1976.

Green, Elmer E., and Green, Alyce M. "The Ins and Outs
of Mind-Body Energy," *Science Year*. pp. 137-147, 1974.

Gunther, Bernard. *Sense Relaxation Below Your Mind*. New York: Collier Books, 1968.

Harmin, Merrill. *How to Get Rid of Emotions that Give You a Pain in the Neck*. Niles, Ill.: Argus Communications, 1976.

Hendricks, Gay, and Wills, Russel. *The Centering Book*. Englewood Cliffs, NJ: Prentice-Hall, Inc., 1975.

Jourand, Sidney M. *Disclosing Man to Himself*. Princeton, NJ: D. Van Nostrand Company, Inc., 1968.

LeCron, L.M. *Self-Hypnotism*. Englewood Cliffs, NJ: Prentice-Hall, 1964.

Leonard, George B. *Education and Ecstacy*. New York: Dell, 1969.

— *The Ultimate Athlete*. New York: Viking Press, 1976.

LeShan, Lawrence. *How to Meditate*. New York: Bantam Books, 1974.

Maslow, A.H. *The Farther Reaches of Human Nature*. New York: The Viking Press, 1971.

Masters, Robert, and Houston, Jean. *Mind Games: The Guide to Inner Space*. New York: Delta/Dell, 1973.

Miller, Lowell G. *Meta-Calisthenics*. New York: Pocket Books, 1976.

Misra, L.K., ed. *Art & Science of Meditation*. Glenview, Ill.: Himalayan Institute, 1976.

Naranjo, Claudio, & Ornstein, Robert E. *On the Psychology of Meditation*. New York: The Viking Press, 1971.

Ornstein, Robert. *The Psychology of Consciousness*. San Francisco, CA.: W.H. Freeman, 1973.

Otis, Leon S. "If Well-Integrated but Anxious, Try TM." *Psychology Today*. Vol. 7, No. 11:45-46, April 1974.

Roberts, Thomas B., ed. *Four Psychologies Applied to Education*. Cambridge, Mass.: Schenkman Publishing Co., 1974.

Rozman, Deborah. *Meditation for Children*. Millbrae, CA.: Celestial Arts, 1976.

Sax, Saville, and Hollander, Sandra. *Wake the Dragon*. Edwardsville, Ill.: Reality Games Institute, 1975.

— *Reality Games*. New York: Popular Library, 1972.

Schrank, Jeffrey. *Teaching Human Beings: 101 Subversive Activities for the Classroom*. Boston: Beacon Press, 1972.

Schutz, William C. *Joy: Expanding Human Awareness*. New York: Grove, 1967.

Schwartz, Gary E. "TM Relaxes Some People and Makes Them Feel Better." *Psychology Today*. Vol. 7, No. 11:39-44, April 1974.

Spolin, Viola. *Improvisation for the Theater*. Evanston, Ill.: Northwestern University Press, 1963.

Stevens, John O. *Awareness: Exploring, Experimenting, Experiencing*. New York: Bantam, 1973.

Suzuki, Shunryu. *Zen Mind, Beginners' Mind*. Philadelphia: Weatherhill, 1970.

Tart, Charles T., ed. *Altered States of Consciousness*. Garden City, New York: Anchor/Doubleday, 1972.

Thera, Nyanaponika. *Power of Mindfulness*. Santa Cruz: Unity, 1972.

White, John, and Fadiman, James, editors. *Relax*.

The man
whose heart and mind are not at rest
is without wisdom
or the power of contemplation;
he who does not practice reflection
hath no calm.
How can a man without calm
obtain happiness?

The Bhagavad-Gita

A Personal Log

Activity	I'll use it	?	Not for me
1. Deep breathing in preparation for work (p. 13)			
2. Complete breathing (p. 14)			
3. Stretching and shaking (p. 17)			
4. Scrunching the body to relax (p. 19)			
5. Tensing and relaxing muscles to relax the body (p. 21)			
6. Using the body sequence to relax the body (p. 23)			

My notes about it

A Personal Log—continued

Activity	I'll use it	?	Not for me
7. Learning to dissolve tension by giving in to it (p. 25)			
8. Mind clearing (p. 33)			
9. A moment apart (p. 35)			
10. What's on your mind? (p. 37)			
11. The memory trip (p. 38)			
12. Clearing emotional energy (p. 40)			

My notes about it

A Personal Log—continued

Activity	I'll use it	?	Not for me
13. Seeing with new eyes (p. 49)			
14. Counting breaths (p. 50)			
15. Repeating a mantra to neutralize thoughts (p. 52)			
16. Here and now wheel (p. 63)			
17. Enlarging awareness (p. 65)			
18. Breathing to regain the center of the self (p. 67)			

My notes about it

A Personal Log—continued

Activity	I'll use it	?	Not for me
19. Rediscovering the whole self (p. 69)			
20. The listening activity (p. 71)			
21. The dream exchange (p. 73)			
22. Sending general messages (p. 80)			
23. The fantasy story (p. 83)			
24. Side-stepping negative energy (p. 84)			

My notes about it